ALBANIAN ENGLISH First Words Picture Book

100 First words Color Picture Book with English Translations

A perfect ALBANIAN English Bilingual First words book!

➢ 28 Color pages, with 100 Words collected and grouped across familiar everyday themes like **family, animals, fruits, vegetables, numbers, colors, home, body parts** and so on

➢ Classic first words are presented in English and ALBANIAN with bright illustrations/photographic color pictures to help with language comprehension

➢ **100 eye-catching** illustrations/ photographs of **familiar things,** each with **big labels color printed underneath in both languages** for easy understanding and comprehension

➢ A great aid for building vocabulary and recognizing words in both languages for all little learners.

➢ Learn ALBANIAN and English language with this bilingual 100 first words book, complete with cheerful COLOR illustrations

➢ An ideal tool to teach new words in both English and ALBANIAN

➢ Fun, educational foreign language introduction for preschoolers and kindergarteners

➢ Premium color cover design

➢ Printed on **high quality** perfectly sized pages at 8.5x11 inches **premium color pages**

D1262572

ALBANIAN Alphabet

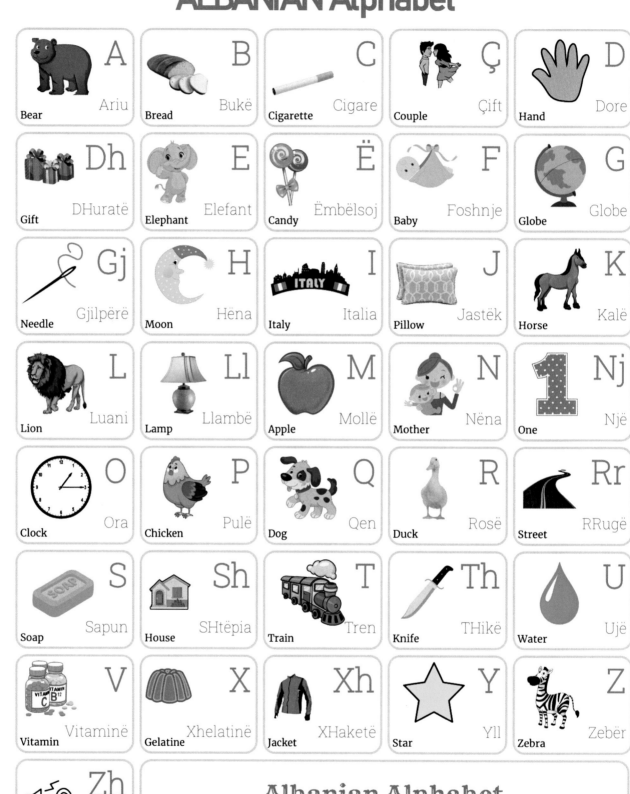

A — Ariu — Bear	B — Bukë — Bread	C — Cigare — Cigarette	Ç — Çift — Couple	D — Dore — Hand
Dh — DHuratë — Gift	E — Elefant — Elephant	Ë — Ëmbëlsoj — Candy	F — Foshnje — Baby	G — Globe — Globe
Gj — Gjilpërë — Needle	H — Hëna — Moon	I — Italia — Italy	J — Jastëk — Pillow	K — Kalë — Horse
L — Luani — Lion	Ll — Llambë — Lamp	M — Mollë — Apple	N — Nëna — Mother	Nj — Një — One
O — Ora — Clock	P — Pulë — Chicken	Q — Qen — Dog	R — Rosë — Duck	Rr — RRugë — Street
S — Sapun — Soap	Sh — SHtëpia — House	T — Tren — Train	Th — THikë — Knife	U — Ujë — Water
V — Vitaminë — Vitamin	X — Xhelatinë — Gelatine	Xh — XHaketë — Jacket	Y — Yll — Star	Z — Zebër — Zebra

Zh — Zhurma — Noise

Albanian Alphabet

Alfabeti Shqip

Fruit

Fruta

Peach

Pjeshkë

Grapes

Rrushi

Orange

Portokalli

Watermelon

Shalqini

Mango

Mango

Banana

Banane

Coconut

Kokosi

Papaya

Papaja

Garlic

Hudhra

Tomato

Domate

Mushroom

Kërpudha

Radish

Rrepkë

Eggplant

Patëllxhan

Pumpkin

Kungull

Cucumber

Kastravec

Animals

Kafshët

Cat

Mace

Dog

Qeni

Fish

Peshku

Lion

Luani

Rabbit

Lepuri

Snake

Gjarpër

Tiger

Tigri

Horse

Kali

Turtle

Breshkë

Donkey

Gomari

Squirrel

Ketri

Elephant

Elefanti

Snail

Kërmilli

Ant

Ant

Frog

Bretkocë

Crab
Gaforrja

Bird
Zog

Hen
Pulë

Cow
Lopë

Butterfly

Flutur

Owl

Buf

Bear

Ariu

Mouse

Miu

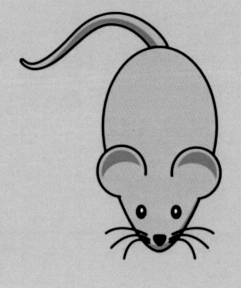

Spider

Merimanga

Parrot

Papagalli

Peacock

Pallua

Pig

Derr

Family

Familja

Father

Babai

Mother

Nëna

Son

Djali

Daughter

E bija

Brother

Vëlla

Sister

Motra

Grandmother

Gjyshja

Baby
Bebe

Grandfather
Gjyshi

Children
Fëmijët

Wife
Gruaja

Socks

Çorape

Button

Butoni

Hat

Kapelë

Shoe

Këpucë

Window

Dritare

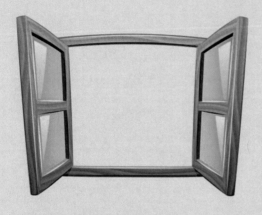

House

Shtëpia

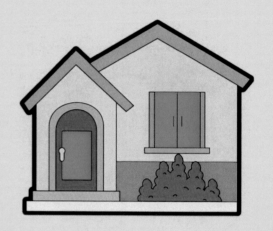

Table

Tabela

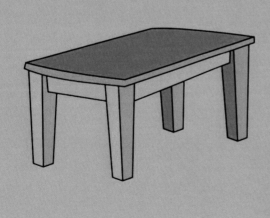

Knife

Thikë

Fever

Ethe

Egg

Vezë

Meat

Mish

Water

Uji

Scissors

Gërshërë

Spoon

Lugë

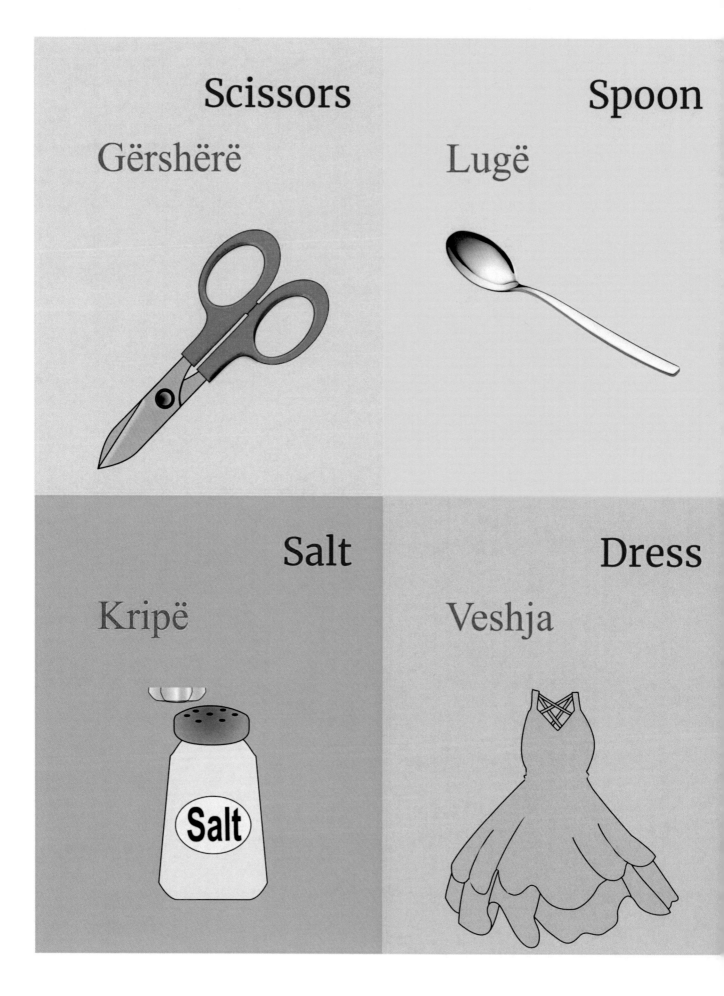

Salt

Kripë

Dress

Veshja

Eye

Syri

Ears

Veshët

Heart

Zemra

Nose

Hunda

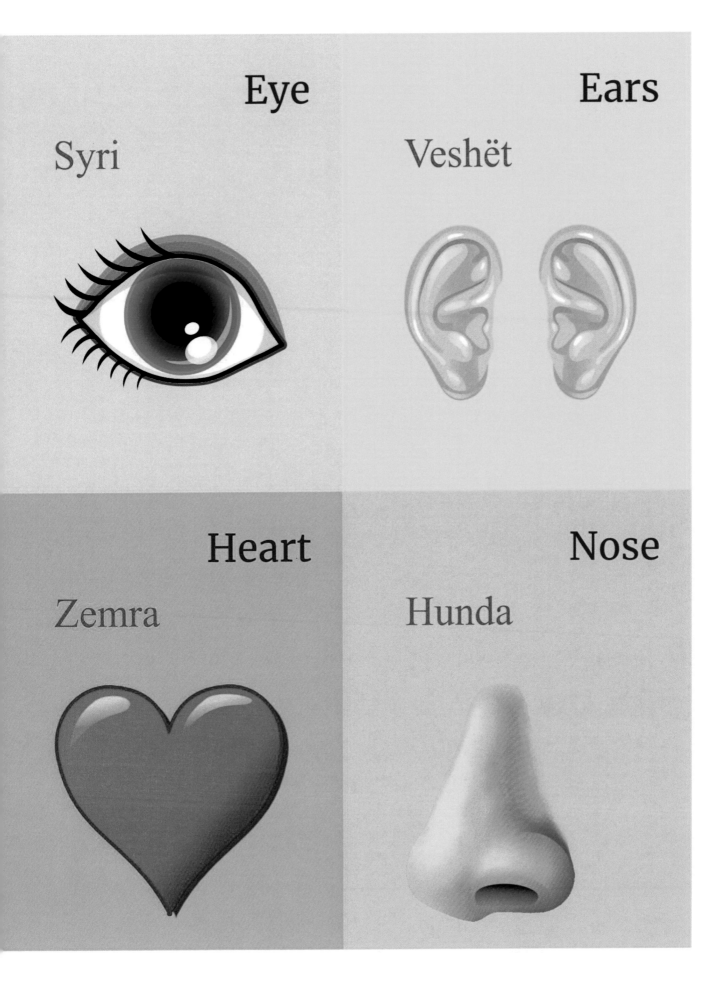

Leg

Këmba

Finger

Gishti

Hair

Flokët

Head

Kokë

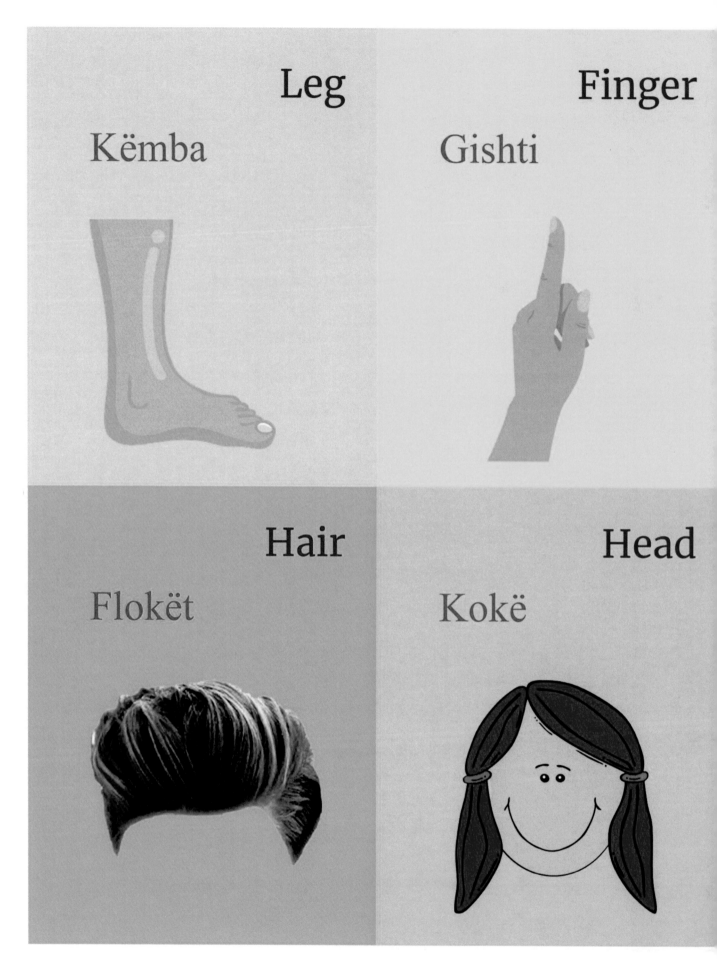

Black

E zezë

Yellow

E verdhe

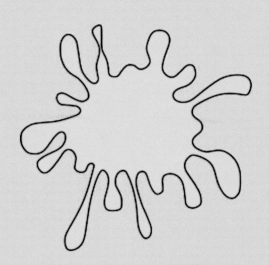

Red

E kuqe

Green

E gjelbër

White

E bardha

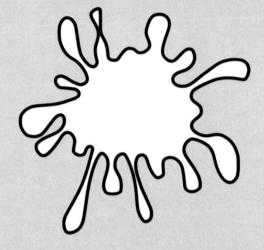

Purple

Vjollcë

Blue

Blu

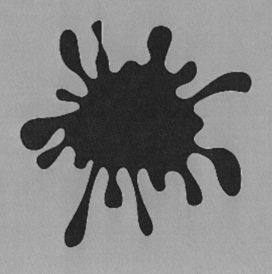

Pink

Rozë

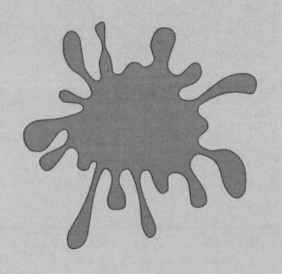

Numbers

Numrat

12345
67890

One

Një

Two

Dy

Three

Tre

Four

Katër

Five

Pesë

Six

Gjashtë

Seven

Shtatë

Eight

Tetë

Nine

Nëntë

Ten

Dhjetë

Twenty

Njëzet

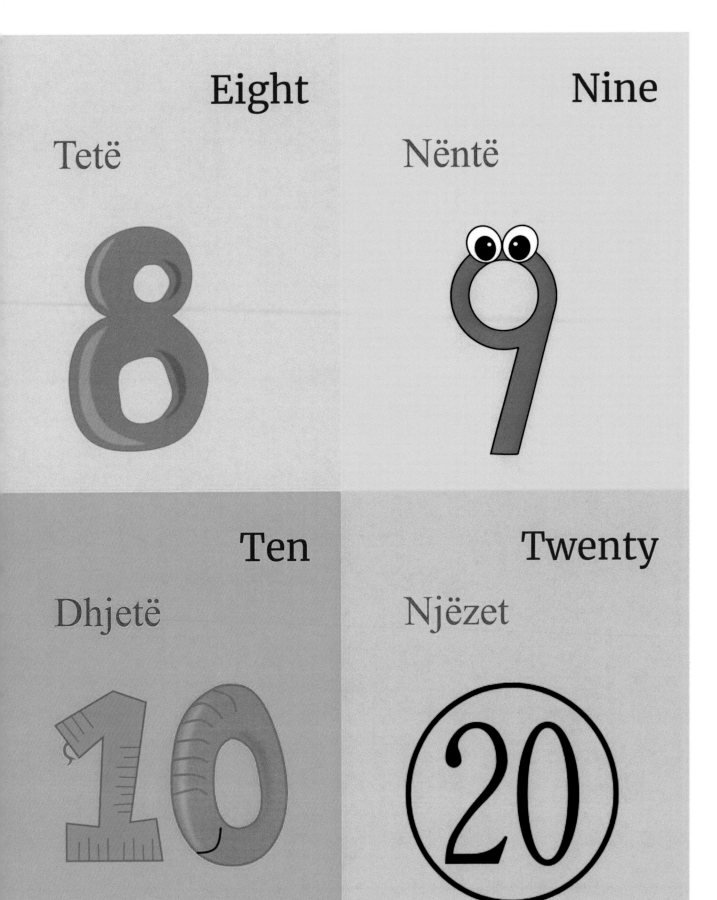

ALBANIAN Alphabet

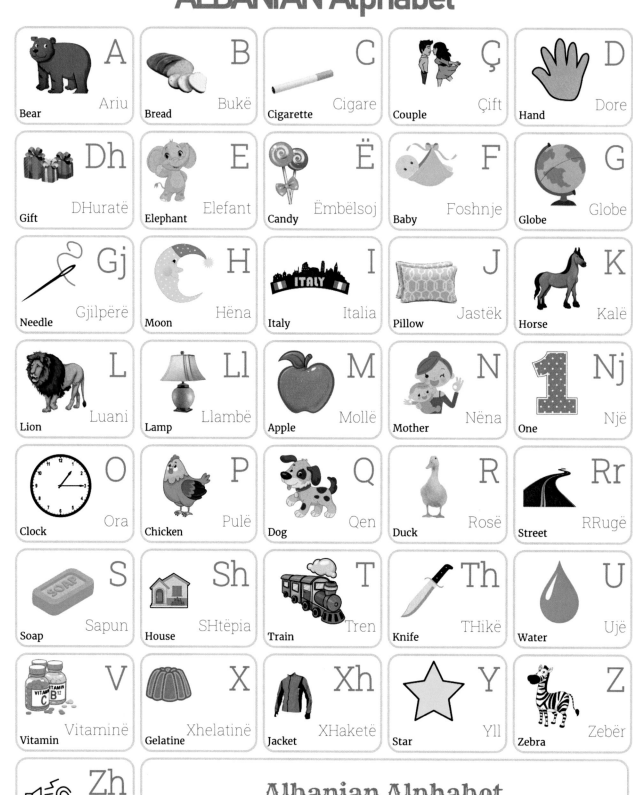

A — Ariu (Bear)	B — Bukë (Bread)	C — Cigare (Cigarette)	Ç — Çift (Couple)	D — Dore (Hand)
Dh — DHuratë (Gift)	E — Elefant (Elephant)	Ë — Ëmbëlsoj (Candy)	F — Foshnje (Baby)	G — Globe (Globe)
Gj — Gjilpërë (Needle)	H — Hëna (Moon)	I — Italia (Italy)	J — Jastëk (Pillow)	K — Kalë (Horse)
L — Luani (Lion)	Ll — Llambë (Lamp)	M — Mollë (Apple)	N — Nëna (Mother)	Nj — Një (One)
O — Ora (Clock)	P — Pulë (Chicken)	Q — Qen (Dog)	R — Rosë (Duck)	Rr — RRugë (Street)
S — Sapun (Soap)	Sh — SHtëpia (House)	T — Tren (Train)	Th — THikë (Knife)	U — Ujë (Water)
V — Vitaminë (Vitamin)	X — Xhelatinë (Gelatine)	Xh — XHaketë (Jacket)	Y — Yll (Star)	Z — Zebër (Zebra)

Zh — Zhurma (Noise)

Albanian Alphabet

Alfabeti Shqip

Made in United States
North Haven, CT
12 April 2023

35338025R00018